SURVIVING
TERROR

TRUE TEEN STORIES FROM
AROUND THE WORLD

True Teen Stories from

MEXICO

Surviving Gangs and the Drug Wars

Derek Miller

Cavendish
Square

New York

Published in 2019 by Cavendish Square Publishing, LLC
243 5th Avenue, Suite 136, New York, NY 10016

First Edition

All websites were available and accurate when this book was sent to press.

Cataloging-in-Publication Data

Names: Miller, Derek.
Title: True teen stories from Mexico: surviving gangs and the drug wars / Derek Miller.
Description: New York : Cavendish Square, 2019. | Series: True teen
stories from around the world | Includes glossary and index.
Identifiers: ISBN 9781502635587 (pbk.) | ISBN 9781502635563
(library bound) | ISBN 9781502635570 (ebook)
Subjects: LCSH: Drug traffic--Mexico. | Drug traffic--Social aspects--Mexico. |
Drug control--Mexico. | Drug dealers--Mexico. | Teenagers--Mexico.
Classification: LCC HV5831.M46 M547 2019 | DDC 363.450972--dc23

Editorial Director: David McNamara
Editor: Caitlyn Miller
Copy Editor: Rebecca Rohan
Associate Art Director: Amy Greenan
Designer: Christina Shults
Production Coordinator: Karol Szymczuk
Photo Research: J8 Media

The photographs in this book are used by permission and through the courtesy of:
Cover Ronaldo Schemidt/AFP/Getty Images p. 4 Dorothy Alexander/Alamy Stock Photo;
p. 11 AFP/Getty Images; p. 18, 80 Alfredo Estrella/AFP/Getty Images; p. 24 Tupungato/
Shuterstock.com; p. 31 Daniel Conejo/AFP/Getty Images; p. 34 Pedro Pardo/AFP/
Getty Images; p. 38 David Monroy/AFP/Getty Images; p. 44 PGR/GDA/Photo Service/
Newscom; p. 47 Hector Guerrero/AFP/Getty Images; p. 51, 56 GDA/AP Images; p. 60
Fernando Brito/AP Photo; p. 63 Tito Herrera/AP Images; p. 66 Incamerastock/Alamy Stock
Photo; p. 69 Elizabeth Ruiz/AFP/Getty Images; p. 76 Mayo 452/Wikimedia Commons/
File:Tierra Caliente en el mapa.jpg/CC BY SA 4.0; p. 84, 93 John Moore/Getty Images.

Printed in the United States of America

CONTENTS

Not all Mexican teens are affected by violence in their country. Here, teens enjoy the Pacific coast.

CHAPTER ONE

GANGS AND CARTELS IN MEXICO

Mexico is a vast country full of contradictions. Large parts of it are scenic, safe, tourist areas—drawing visitors from around the world to experience Mexico's vibrant culture and beautiful beaches. But some areas are wracked by high levels of violence. Fueled largely by the insatiable demand for drugs in the United States, massive cartels have infiltrated Mexico. To get their share of the lucrative drug trade, they commit acts of heinous violence. Cartels target each other, civilians, law enforcement, and anyone else unlucky enough to get in their way.

Victims are not limited to Mexican citizens—who do make up the majority of those affected—but also include many United States citizens. Americans, both in Mexico and in the United States, are often caught up in the violence. Innocent Americans traveling in Mexico or living near the border are affected, as are American law enforcement officers. Furthermore, Americans are often recruited by cartels run out of Mexico to commit crimes on that cartel's behalf.

Criminal activity in Mexico affects the lives of ordinary Mexicans on a massive scale. Violence among cartels and gangs is a constant threat in many cities. Citizens often have to check the news and social media before even venturing out of their homes so that they know where violent clashes are occurring. Gun battles can necessitate taking a different route to school or church.

But being harmed in a violent clash between rival armed groups is not the only danger. Gangs and cartels also target ordinary citizens in a variety of crimes. From robbery to extorting protection money from local businesses, Mexican people are often forced to give their money to criminals.

Additionally, Mexican civilians must also watch out for their children. Criminal groups often recruit children to their illegal enterprises; many are not even teenagers when they are first approached. Child recruits are rarely given a choice about helping a cartel. They either help or they, and their families, face violent consequences.

A Billion Dollar Industry

Organized crime in Mexico is fueled by the huge American market for illegal drugs. The United States is the largest consumer of illicit drugs in the world. Each year, Americans in the US spend more than $100 billion on drugs. Most of these drugs are produced overseas and smuggled into the country. Mexico is an important production and transit route for most types of narcotics. Marijuana is grown in the country before being shipped north. The opium poppy, a plant used to manufacture heroin, is also grown there. Illicit labs then process the opium into heroin and smuggle it across the border. Since the early 1990s, labs in Mexico have also produced methamphetamine for US markets. While cocaine is manufactured in South America, where the climate is more suitable for growing the source plant, coca, some of it is then shipped to Mexico. From Mexico, it crosses the border into the United States.

While huge amounts of illegal drugs are trafficked through Mexico, it is not the only source for any of them. Heroin, methamphetamine, and other drugs also find their way into the United States from ports and across the Canadian border. In fact, in 2016, more than 90 percent of the ecstasy seized upon entry to the United States was at the Canadian border. However, a staggering 99 percent of marijuana, methamphetamine, and heroin seized were confiscated at the Mexican border. Most cocaine was seized at ports in California, but 38 percent was at the Mexican border.

The primary tool that the United States uses to estimate where drugs come from is the amounts seized at various borders. Naturally, this is not an exact science. A porous border might simply allow more drugs through, making it appear that there is little traffic when in fact it is just harder to stop drugs there.

Similarly, the amount of money that flows from the United States into Mexico due to the drug trade is difficult to know. However, according to one Mexican official in early 2017, it is estimated at $64 billion a year. In 2013, the US State Department estimated a more modest $19 to $29 billion. Whatever the exact number, there is no doubt that cartel bosses live extravagant lifestyles that few in the world can match. It is not uncommon for police to find millions of dollars in cash when bosses are captured—as well as luxury cars, planes, and mansions.

These riches derive from money that Americans pay for drugs from Mexico. According to the 2016 National Survey on Drug Use and Health, an astonishing 10.6 percent of Americans over the age of twelve had used illegal drugs in the past month. Most of this is accounted for by marijuana and the misuse of prescription medication such as painkillers and tranquilizers. But 0.2 percent of the population reported using heroin in the last month. The number was the same for methamphetamine, and even higher at 0.7 percent for cocaine. Not only does this rampant drug use cause health issues in the United States, it also inspires violence both north and south of the Mexican-American border.

Many victims of drug violence are innocent bystanders who were simply in the wrong place at the wrong time. While traveling to some parts of Mexico is advised against by agencies like the US Department of State, many popular tourist areas are considered safe. The chance of drug violence is low, but just like on the streets of any American city, it is still possible.

Early in the morning of January 16, 2017, tragedy struck the resort city of Playa del Carmen. Up until 2017, the area, with its large number of resorts and tourists, had been considered largely unscathed by violence from organized crime. That changed when a gunman opened fire at a club hosting a large, international music festival. The shots inspired a stampede of people desperate to escape the flying bullets. They did not know whether it was a terror attack, so many fled the building and tried to climb a large fence that was difficult to scale. The resulting stampede caused many more injuries.

EL CHAPO

The most notorious drug lord of recent years was born Joaquín Archivaldo Guzmán Loera to an average family in Sinaloa. Today, he is more commonly called "El Chapo" ("Shorty" in Spanish). From a young age, Guzmán became involved with the production of drugs, growing marijuana and harvesting opium. He eventually became involved with the Guadalajara cartel and oversaw a smuggling route across the US border.

When the head of the Guadalajara cartel was arrested, Guzmán ran a part of the empire before striking out on his own. He became the unquestioned leader of the Sinaloa cartel. Over time, it became the largest, most effective cartel in Mexico— despite the repeated arrests of Guzmán.

In 1993, Guzmán was arrested for the first time. His brother led the cartel outside of prison, and Guzmán managed operations from inside. However, in 2001, he escaped from prison in a laundry cart with the help of prison officials. The combination of money—and threats—from one of the most powerful men in the world was difficult for the officials to resist. In 2014, Guzmán was finally recaptured, but only one year later, he once again escaped. This time, it was through a massive tunnel leading outside from the shower in his cell.

Guzmán in prison after his first capture by authorities in 1993

Finally, in 2016, he was captured for the third time and later extradited to the United States, where it is hoped he cannot escape once more. His long tenure as the most powerful—and richest—drug lord in the world as well as his two spectacular escapes from high-security prisons have made Guzmán famous around the world.

In the end, five people were killed, including tourists from Italy, Mexico, and the United States as well as two employees of the festival, one Canadian and one Mexican. The American victim was eighteen-year-old Alejandra Villanueva Ibarra from Denver, Colorado. She was killed during the panicked stampede of people toward the exits. Ibarra was the caregiver of her two younger siblings and supported her family financially. She was also attending school to be a teacher of students with special needs, but her promising life was cut short by indiscriminate violence.

Police think the shooting was likely perpetrated by Los Zetas, a major drug trafficking organization in Mexico. Blankets were strung up around the city after the shooting with a message allegedly from Los Zetas written on them. It said that the shooting was due to the refusal of the event organizers to pay money to the cartel, although the authenticity of those messages is difficult to confirm.

In addition to bystanders, cartel members themselves are often subject to brutal violence. Many of them are forced to join the criminal organization from a young age—and never reach adulthood. This was true in the case of Jose Armando Moreno. In 2013, the thirteen-year-old boy was arrested by the police. He confessed to being involved in ten murders and personally committing three on behalf of Los Zetas. A troubled child, he had left home at the age of eleven. Because it is illegal in Mexico to imprison children under the age of fourteen, Moreno was released despite his confession.

Three weeks later, the bodies of six people were found on the side of a highway. They had been tortured and executed. The bodies of Moreno and his mother were among them. Like most murders in Mexico, the case was never solved. But it is likely that Moreno's confession to the police sealed his fate. His young age saved him from prison, but not from the people for whom he had killed.

The Rise of Cartels

The word "cartel" is often used to describe the vast criminal networks engaged in drug smuggling in Mexico and South America. However, academics have generally avoided the term. Cartels are groups of producers that control the price of a product by working together. They might do this by restricting the supply—leading to higher prices—or simply fixing the price at a certain level. If no one else can produce the product, this can lead to higher profits for everyone. It is generally against the law for legitimate businesses to do this.

Drug cartels have never been true cartels in this sense of the word. They generally flood the market with illicit drugs and do not cooperate with one another to fix prices. As a result, academics typically call cartels "drug trafficking organizations" (DTOs). They are also sometimes called organized crime groups (OCGs)—to recognize that they make money through more than just drug trafficking. The term "OCG" focuses on their vast size and reach.

Nevertheless, since the 1980s, DTOs have been called cartels in the media and by the public. The term was first used to describe Pablo Escobar's Medellin cartel, a cocaine-trafficking organization that was likely the first DTO to make its leader a multibillionaire.

For years, Escobar was untouchable in Colombia. He served a brief stint as a congressman—as well as organizing an armed siege of the Colombian Supreme Court building and bombing a passenger plane full of people. He finally surrendered to authorities on the condition that he could build his own luxury prison, which he soon escaped from.

After years of terrorizing the country (the term "narcoterrorist" was even coined in his honor), Escobar was brought down by a coalition of his enemies. Colombian authorities, with the help of the DEA and information from rival drug bosses, found him, and he was killed in a shootout. However, he had already defined a new kind of cartel kingpin—one that was more powerful than the government and above the law.

A phrase that came to be associated with Escobar's powerful reach was "plata o plomo" ("silver or lead"). The police and government officials were given a choice—take a bribe or be killed. Either way, Escobar remained above the law. It was a path that other cartel leaders soon followed.

Drug Trafficking Organizations and Gangs

It is important to distinguish DTOs like those run by Escobar and Guzmán from youth gangs. Often, these two groups are thought of as the same thing. Members of both are labeled "gang members." However, there are massive differences between DTOs and youth gangs.

Youth gangs tend to be made up of a couple hundred members at most and usually quite a few less. They are generally local phenomena, where youths from an area band together in an unorganized way. The hierarchy is flat, without authoritarian figures at the top. According to the Organization of American States, youth gangs are:

> a spontaneous effort by children and young people to create, where it does not exist, an urban space in society that is adapted to their needs, where they can exercise the rights that their families, government, and communities do not offer them. Arising out of extreme poverty, exclusion, and a lack of opportunities, gangs

THE DRUG ENFORCEMENT AGENCY

The Drug Enforcement Agency (DEA) was founded in 1973. Its mission is "to enforce the controlled substances laws and regulations of the United States" by bringing traffickers to justice both in the United States and abroad. It has field offices across the United States and in many foreign countries to aid foreign governments in their fight against drug traffickers.

The history of the DEA in Mexico is defined by an event in 1985. While the agency was focusing on the massive cocaine trade in Colombia, an agent, Enrique "Kiki" Camarena, was kidnapped from a field office in Guadalajara, Mexico. The Guadalajara cartel (of which El Chapo was a mid-level member at the time) had decided Camarena was responsible for a major bust. The cartel retaliated by torturing and killing him.

The DEA responded with the largest homicide investigation of its history until that point. It went after the cartel and arrested its leaders over the following years. Camarena's murder had been a huge mistake. Mexico's cartels went from being a low priority to a major mission of the DEA after his death.

Today, the DEA is still heavily involved in Mexico. They provide intelligence to the Mexican police and are involved in many major operations targeting cartel leaders. The CIA (Central Intelligence Agency) and American civilian military contractors also aid the Mexican government in its war on the cartels.

try to gain their rights and meet their needs by organizing themselves without supervision and developing their own rules, and by securing for themselves a territory and a set of symbols that gives meaning to their membership in the group. This endeavor to exercise their citizenship is, in many cases, a violation of their own and others' rights, and frequently generates violence and crime in a vicious circle that perpetuates their original exclusion.

DTOs different from youth gangs in several key ways. Youth gangs engage in crime (or else they would not be called a gang), but of a different sort than DTOs. They typically distribute drugs to their local area and extort local businesses. They lack the massive reach and huge profits, often in the billions of dollars, of DTOs.

DTOs are also much larger and have many more members. Their organization is often compared to those of multinational corporations rather than of street gangs. The leader has complete control of operations like a business's CEO, and there is a strict hierarchy of power and organization. While reading the stories of teen recruits and victims of both DTOs and gangs, it is important to know that there is a substantial difference between the two types of groups.

Soldiers in the Mexican Army participate in an operation against drug traffickers.

CHAPTER TWO

A CLOSER LOOK AT MEXICO AND THE RISE OF VIOLENCE

The history of illegal trafficking has a long history in Mexico. Early in the twentieth century, the United States passed an amendment banning the sale of alcohol. This ushered in the Prohibition era. Despite the law, Americans continued to drink alcohol. Prohibition's major effect was to fuel the rise of criminal organizations that saw massive profits from manufacturing and smuggling alcohol across the United States. This was the time when the Mafia, led by people like Al Capone, got their start—making a profit from Prohibition.

In fact, the first Mexican cartel began in this era by smuggling alcohol into the United States. It later turned to marijuana after alcohol was made legal once again. While the American government admitted that alcohol prohibition was a failure and reversed it, the prohibition of drugs increased over the coming years. Today, the early cartel still exists under the name the Gulf cartel—a major DTO.

The modern history of drug trafficking largely began in the 1980s. After Colombian drug trafficker Pablo Escobar began using Mexico to smuggle cocaine into the United States, many different Mexican cartels sprang up to get their share of the profits. For a time, they were largely ignored by the Mexican government. However, this changed in 2006 when Felipe Calderón became president of Mexico.

The Mexican Drug War

Calderón initiated what has become known as the Mexican Drug War with a large-scale offensive against the cartels. Using not only the federal police, but also the Mexican military, Calderón waged an all-out war against the cartels. Unlike the United States' War on Drugs (which is largely run by law-enforcement officers), the Mexican Drug War truly earned the label "war." The military went into areas armed to the teeth, trying to shut down cartels that were themselves armed more like a country's armed forces than a criminal organization.

There have been countless clashes between cartels and the Mexican government's forces. They often play out more like firefights in a war than the arrest of criminals. In one example, on September 30, 2016, a military convoy was ambushed by cartel gunmen armed with automatic weapons and grenades. Six soldiers were killed, and two military Humvees were destroyed. Weeks earlier, a police helicopter that was trying to support law enforcement officers engaged in a gun battle was shot out of the sky by cartel gunmen. Mexican forces responded in kind. In February of 2017, a leader of the Beltrán Leyva drug cartel and eleven of his underlings were killed when a military helicopter poured machine gun fire into their house from above.

The Rising Tide of Violence

One unintended consequence of the Mexican Drug War was a major uptick in violence across the country. Not only did the Mexican government and cartels clash, but the war also created a rise in violence between cartels. Mexican civilians were caught in the crossfire and died in greater numbers than ever before.

While Mexico does not keep a record of deaths due to drug violence (often the exact reasons for a murder are unclear to begin with), the country does log the number of murders committed. At the beginning of the Drug War, there were roughly 8.1 murders per 100,000 people in Mexico each year. Compare that to the murder rate of 5.6 per 100,000 people in the United States in 2016 or the rate of Louisiana—the state with the highest murder rate—at 11.8 in the same year. Mexico's murder rate was not extraordinarily high at that time, but it quickly spiked. By 2011, the murder rate in Mexico was 24 per 100,000 people—nearly triple the rate of just five years earlier at the outbreak of the Mexican Drug War. There is no doubt the higher rate was due to increased violence associated with the struggle over drug trafficking.

Since the Mexican Drug War began at the end of 2006, more than 100,000 Mexicans have died in drug-related violence. This is a staggering number of people. It is more than thirty-three times the number of people who died in the September 11, 2001 terror attacks in the United States. In fact, there is no event or war in recent American history that compares until you look all the way back to World War II in the early 1940s.

The Balkanization of the Cartels

While the murder rate in Mexico reached a peak in 2011, it began to decline quite quickly. It reached a temporary low in 2014, when it was at 17.1 per 100,000—a major decrease from the high of 2011, although still much higher than before the Mexican Drug War began.

Strangely enough, this reduction in violence was likely due to the unchallenged power of the Sinaloa cartel, led by El Chapo. In the violent clashes that occurred between the cartels, the Sinaloa cartel came out on top. It took control of huge amounts of territory, including prime locations on the US border for major smuggling routes.

Many analysts and journalists have suggested that there was also a level of complicity between the Sinaloa cartel and the government of Calderón. Government forces largely ignored Guzmán and his cartel in favor of cracking down on his competitors. This allowed the Sinaloa cartel to consolidate power and led to a large decrease in violence in their sprawling territory. Without the need to fight other cartels or the government, an era of relative peace and stability was ushered in. It has been called the Pax Sinaloa (named after the Pax Romana—"Roman peace"—that was a long period of peace under the rule of the Roman Empire).

This changed with the third arrest of Guzmán in early 2016. The king was finally gone—likely for good, as extradition to the United States loomed and was eventually accomplished. Intense violence broke out as cartels scrambled to fill the power vacuum.

LIFE AMIDST THE VIOLENCE

Drug violence in Mexico has a tangible effect on daily life for millions of ordinary people across the country. This is especially pronounced in areas that are prone to drug trafficking and drug production.

One city that suffers terribly from drug trafficking and the violence that accompanies it is Ciudad Juárez. It is the largest city in the Mexican state of Chihuahua, right on the border of Texas. The only thing that separates Ciudad Juárez and the

Ciudad Juárez lies on the American border.

Texan city of El Paso is the Rio Grande, but life on the two sides of the river could not be more different. Drug violence is an ever-present threat in Juárez. It has been an epicenter of violence due to its prime location on the American border. While the city saw a brief lull in violence in 2015, the homicide rate doubled in 2016 with a new war between competing cartels.

In 2009, Mexican teen Marina Diaz spoke with CNN about life in the city. She attended school every day in El Paso, Texas. Her parents were willing to pay the steep price for private school tuition there so that she could learn safely, away from the violence on the Mexican side of the border.

Diaz recalled the first time she had seen a dead body in the street in Juárez. It was surrounded by a crowd of people: "They told us that it had happened just a few minutes before, and it was like, wow, if we were there only a few minutes earlier, maybe it could've been us." Despite the dangers she faced every day going to El Paso, she was most worried about her father. She said, "I think that especially my dad, he's the one who works, he's a salesman, he works in the streets, he has to visit his clients, has to offer his products, so most of his time is on the streets driving and that's a big cause of stress because anything might happen." In Juárez, the constant violence is always a concern.

The chaos was compounded by the government's efforts over the past decade. They followed the so-called kingpin strategy (as the United States had in earlier years in Colombia). The leaders of cartels were targeted for arrest. It was an obvious weak point for the government to go after— leaders could be captured once and for all (if you overlooked their ability to escape from prison). Going after smuggling routes and manufacturing centers was much less definitive. Infrastructure could simply be recreated somewhere else under the direction of cartel leaders.

The unfortunate outcome of the kingpin strategy was a proliferation of cartels that quickly came into conflict with one another. It is often referred to as the balkanization of the cartels. (This is a reference to the splintering of the Balkans region of Europe into many smaller countries.)

When cartel leaders like Guzmán were arrested, the large number of heavily armed, hardened criminals under them did not disappear. They simply organized themselves in smaller groups if no one person was influential enough to fill the shoes of the cartel leader. While organizations like the Sinaloa cartel continue to exist, many smaller groups often carved out territory when the leader was imprisoned. In many cases, neighboring cartels also seized the opportunity to encroach on their territory in the chaos—causing even more violence.

The Situation Today

The balkanization of the cartels was largely a disaster for the Mexican people. While Guzmán preferred the multibillion-dollar business of drug trafficking, many of the small armed groups that rose up after his downfall were not happy with their small slice of the drug-trafficking pie. As a result, they turned to kidnapping and extortion to make money.

Due to this splintering of the cartels, violence in Mexico has increased dramatically since Guzmán's most recent arrest. The year 2017 was the deadliest year since Mexico began keeping central records of murders in 1997. In the first eleven months, the number of murders surpassed the entire previous record year of 2011.

According to a US Congressional report published in April 2017, there were just four major DTOs at the beginning of the Mexican Drug War. That number increased to between nine and twenty by the time the report was published a decade later—and that does not include the many smaller factions that arose. The Sinaloa cartel remains one of the top cartels even after Guzmán's extradition. The following DTOs are some of the most prominent that are often mentioned in the news.

Los Zetas

The history of Los Zetas begins in the 1990s. At that time, they were part of the Gulf cartel. Their leadership and many of their members were highly trained ex–airborne special forces from the Mexican army. They became enforcers and assassins for the old and powerful Gulf cartel for the promise of more money than they could ever make working for the government. They earned a reputation for extreme brutality and were more heavily involved in kidnapping, extortion, and human trafficking than most DTOs.

In 2010, Los Zetas decided that there was even more opportunity for riches if they were free agents. They broke away from the Gulf cartel, sparking a civil war within the DTO. They seized vast swaths of territory from the Gulf cartel and its neighbors. By 2012, Los Zetas controlled more territory than any other DTO in Mexico. While a series of arrests removed many of their leaders between 2012 and 2015, they remain a powerful DTO. They are often in the news for leaving messages to the government and media along with corpses in plain sight.

Jalisco New Generation Cartel (Cartel Jalisco Nueva Generación, or CJNG)

As its name implies, CJNG is part of a new breed of DTO. It was originally called the Zeta Killers, and it announced its formation by displaying thirty-five bodies of people it said were members of Los Zetas. At this point, it was likely part of the Sinaloa cartel, although it soon went to war with them as well as Los Zetas and the Gulf cartel for more territory. In 2015, the Mexican government labeled it one of the two most dangerous DTOs in the country along with the Sinaloa DTO.

CJNG is notable for its refusal to play by any rules. It was responsible for shooting down a government helicopter and singling out many high-ranking government officials for acts of violence. It also took over the resort town of Acapulco and interfered with international tourism in the region. CJNG's flagrant disregard for playing by the rules that even other DTOs often follow has led to it being heavily targeted by the government. Its leader, "El Mencho," has a $5 million reward on his head for information leading to his capture that was issued by the US government.

Crossing the Border

Mexico's prominent role in the world of drug trafficking is due in part to its massive land border with the United States. But despite this border, it is not easy for drugs to find their way from Mexico into the United States. The American government spends billions of dollars each year to protect the border and prevent both drugs and undocumented immigrants from crossing the border illegally.

The border is secured in a number of ways along its 1,989 miles (3,200 km). At some parts, there are physical walls, or fences, that prevent people from crossing easily. Along roads and highways, there are secured border checkpoints where agents search and screen arrivals, who are required to have the proper documents. In other areas, the physical geography itself forms the border—vast deserts and the Rio Grande are sometimes the only barrier to crossing.

Nevertheless, these security measures have proven fruitless. Drug—and human—traffickers have many techniques they use to cross the border. To smuggle drugs, many techniques involve very simple but practical ways to cross a fence or wall. Rudimentary catapults are used to hurl drugs across the border with someone on the other side waiting to simply pick them off the ground. More recently, commercially available drones are flown across the border with drugs attached to them. While border agents intercept some packages sent in this manner, many are picked up by drug traffickers without a hitch. Ladders or ropes are used by people to scale the walls and fences, often in a matter of seconds, even at the most secured points.

One of the more complex ways to smuggle drugs and people across the border is through tunnels. The Sinaloa cartel was responsible for building the first drug-smuggling tunnel under the border in 1989. Since then, many other DTOs have followed their lead. The tunnels can stretch as far as half a mile underground. Their entrances and exits are often hidden in buildings on either side of the border. The tunnels themselves range in complexity. Some are merely holes dug through the earth. Others have elevators, electric lights, ventilation systems, and rails that expedite the movement of huge quantities of drugs. Regardless of security features at the surface, tunnels give DTOs the means to move massive quantities of drugs across the border in a short time frame. Using private airplanes and boats to avoid border security at all is still a popular method too.

This photo shows an uncompleted border tunnel that authorities found in Tijuana.

In 2016, 30 percent of the drugs confiscated at the border were at secured border crossings. The drugs are hidden in cars and trucks that then attempt to cross the border. They blend in with the tens of millions of legal border crossings that occur each year—making them very difficult to stop. Given the vast quantity of drugs that enter the country in this way, it is clear the DTOs consider it a mainstay.

The major consequence of increased security at the border has been the creation of a criminal enterprise devoted to thwarting American efforts to shut down both drug and human trafficking. One trafficker interviewed by Ioan Grillo for the *New York Times* recalled that he charged just 50 cents to ferry someone across the border in 1984. In 2017, he charged $5,000 due to the increased difficulty. This money is largely routed to the very same DTOs that are responsible for drug trafficking and violence.

The Heroin Epidemic

In recent years, American officials have begun to focus on the heroin epidemic gripping the country. The number of Americans overdosing on the drug has risen dramatically since 2010, year after year. In 2017, the number of heroin overdoses had quadrupled since 2010. There are a few major reasons for this change.

Beginning at the end of 2012, two states—Colorado and Washington—legalized the sale of marijuana for recreational use. Since then, many other states have followed. Proponents argue that this is a large step forward for personal freedom as well as a potential source of tax revenue for the government. Opponents say marijuana is a harmful drug and legalization will increase its availability. However you view the issue, the recent move toward legalization has had a massive effect on Mexican DTOs. Marijuana had always been one of their major sources of income. The country's climate is suited for its cultivation, and the United States has always had a huge appetite for the drug. With the wave of legalization, business for the cartels suffered terribly. Higher-quality marijuana is now grown domestically in the United States by companies that do not need to smuggle it across borders, pay enforcers, or bribe officials.

The cartels of Mexico responded by focusing on production of their other major cash sources: heroin and fentanyl. These two drugs are opioid painkillers—the same as many other prescription medications such as morphine, oxycodone, and the active ingredients in pharmaceuticals like Vicodin and Oxycontin. In small doses, they manage pain. In large doses, they cause euphoria, making them a popular, yet dangerous, recreational drug.

Heroin is produced from the sap-like opium that leaks out of cut opium poppies.

The rising popularity of opioids in recent years was largely due to prescription medications that contained them. Prescriptions would be diverted through fraud and theft to the illegal market. People who were prescribed opioids for legitimate complaints also became addicted. When a prescription ran out, some would turn to buying them illegally. Since heroin has much of the same effects as prescription painkillers—it is just stronger—people addicted to prescription pills sometimes turn to it for relief from the painful symptoms of withdrawal. Heroin is also much cheaper than the equivalent dose in prescription form.

The ramping up of Mexican production of heroin and fentanyl corresponded to the DEA crackdown on opioid prescriptions. Doctors were encouraged not to hand them out as frequently. Those already addicted were forced to turn to street drugs. Fentanyl also became a boon for the drug cartels. Much more powerful than heroin, it was more cost-effective to smuggle it across borders. Furthermore, fentanyl is made in a lab rather than harvested from the opium poppy. This makes it harder for the government to combat production. There are no vast fields to target, and any building can be converted to a lab.

The result of all those factors was the heroin (and fentanyl) epidemic that has swept across the United States in recent years. Never before has the number of drug overdoses been as high as it currently is. In 2016, the CDC estimates sixty-four thousand Americans died from drug overdoses, which is a 19 percent increase from 2015. More Americans died from drug overdoses than from car accidents or guns. More than 80 percent of those deaths were from opioids. The biggest offender was fentanyl. The extreme potency of fentanyl makes it extremely risky to take. While heroin is typically 35 to 50 percent pure, fentanyl must be cut to single-digit purities. This makes it much less forgiving if any drug dealer fails to cut it properly. A small variation in purity can be the difference between living and dying when it is used.

Nineteen-year-old Jonathan Ledbetter of Cleveland County, North Carolina, is one American teen who suffered the ultimate cost of fentanyl's danger. He struggled with drug addiction but wanted to quit. On November 7, 2017, he overdosed on fentanyl. His father Joel recalled that, "He spent that whole week working on his application to get into rehab, running around telling everybody, 'I'm going to get better, I'm going to get better. I love you, I'll see you when I get back,' and that was his goal." Four days after overdosing, Jonathan passed away. His father shared the family's story with the media in the hopes that it may help spread awareness of the dangers—and heavy cost—of drug addiction.

THE RICHEST MAN IN MEXICO

The drug trade involves enormous sums of money, yet the sixth-richest man in the world in 2017 lives in Mexico and earned his wealth through honest hard work. Carlos Slim Helu is involved in many different businesses across the country. His parents emigrated to Mexico from modern-day Lebanon in the early twentieth century. When the Mexican Revolution broke out, Slim's father bought real estate at low prices due to the violence and instability. He made massive profits on his real-estate investments.

Carlos Slim was born in 1940 and became involved in his father's businesses at a young age. He also began to invest on his own. When he was just eleven years old, he bought savings bonds and tracked the performance of his investments. When the Mexican economy experienced problems in the 1980s and stock prices dropped, Slim took a page from his father's playbook and bought stocks at rock-bottom prices. When they rose later, he became extraordinarily wealthy. He used his money to invest heavily in telecommunications, an industry he still dominates in Mexico.

As of January 18, 2018, Forbes estimates Slim's net worth at $69 billion. His entrepreneurial spirit and a work ethic that began in his childhood and continued through his teenage years had paid off.

Police officers and soldiers who deal with cartel members wear balaclavas to protect their identities—and the lives of themselves and their families.

CHAPTER THREE

TEEN RECRUITS

Mexican DTO and gang members are young people for the most part. Just a couple decades ago, new recruits in Mexican DTOs were twenty years old on average. Today, it is commonplace for pre-teen children to be recruited into DTOs. Boys and girls between twelve and fifteen years of age are encouraged to drop out school and work for criminal organizations. Children and teens are often promised more money than they could ever hope to make otherwise, but in reality, they are more likely to lose their lives than to strike it rich.

Children are the preferred recruits for DTOs for a number of reasons. They are easier to convince to commit crimes since they do not think about the consequences of their actions as much as adults. Furthermore, anyone under the age of fourteen is immune from prosecution for crimes according to the Mexican constitution. This immunity is not unique to Mexico—most countries subscribe to international agreements that protect children under the age of fifteen from being prosecuted for war crimes. The reasoning is that child soldiers or gang members are victims themselves and not responsible for the crimes they are forced to commit. Unfortunately, this immunity encourages the recruitment of children to some degree.

While some of the low-level soldiers and many of the drug mules in Mexican DTOs are children, most of the leadership is composed of older men and women. Though most DTO bosses are men, some women do rise to positions of leadership. Girls and women also commonly fulfill low level roles as drug mules and *sicarios*—the Spanish word for killer that typically refers to cartel gunmen and assassins.

Today, tens of thousands of children and teens work for Mexican DTOs. Many more are members of Mexican street gangs. In this chapter, we will look at the stories of a few of these teen recruits.

El Ponchis: Child Soldier

No case spotlights the issue of children being recruited to DTOs more than that of El Ponchis. In 2010, a fourteen-year-old Mexican boy tried to fly to Tijuana, a Mexican city on the border with California. He and his sister hoped to cross the border and live with their mother in San Diego. Instead, they were arrested by Mexican authorities.

The pair was interrogated and made a series of confessions that shocked the world. El Ponchis, a diminutive boy, admitted to killing four people on behalf of a DTO—the cartel of the South Pacific. He later recounted on camera how this period of his life began, "When I was eleven, they picked me up. They said they would kill me ... I've killed four people, decapitated them. I felt bad doing it. They made me. They said if I didn't do it, they would kill me."

The beginnings to some of the murders were captured on video in El Ponchis's phone. The videos show him beating the victims who later turned up dead. El Ponchis worked in a cell that included his sister and other cartel killers. At first, they were paid $2,500 for a murder. That price later increased to $3,000. The dead bodies of the victims were dumped by the side of the road or hung from overpasses—a common method Mexican DTOs use to instill terror.

El Ponchis also reported that, like many child soldiers around the globe, he was given drugs before he committed acts of violence. These served to mask his fear and allow him to do the terrible things he was ordered to do. Other DTO members who were part of the same group as El Ponchis alleged that he was also responsible for mutilating the bodies of victims, cutting off many body parts from the corpses. It is a charge that El Ponchis denied and refused to confess to.

After his confession, El Ponchis was sentenced to just three years in custody, the maximum sentence possible for someone his age in Mexico. The short sentence shocked many people around the world who wanted a harsher sentence despite his young age. El Ponchis himself said, "I know what will happen to me now. I regret getting involved in this and killing people. But when I'm released, I want to go straight. I'll work, do anything, as long as it's not a return to this."

After three years of rehabilitation in Mexico, El Ponchis was flown to San Antonio when he was released. Born in San Diego, he was an American citizen, and despite committing four murders, he was now a free seventeen-year-old in the United States. His previous life in the States had been difficult. He was taken away at birth from his parents because cocaine was detected in his system; his mother had been using shortly before going into labor. He was put into foster care as a result. His mother and father were both heavy users of illegal drugs and violent with one another.

He and his siblings were eventually taken in by his grandmother in Cuernavaca, Mexico, when El Ponchis was eighteen months old. They lived a good life there and stayed out of trouble. His second-grade gym teacher recalled that, "At that age he wasn't taking drugs. He was a good-natured but abandoned kid." But that changed when their grandmother died. He and his sister lived rough lives before being recruited into the DTO. After their recruitment, they lived in a small concrete house that served as a home for many DTO members. Since his release in 2013, El Ponchis has kept a low profile. There has been no coverage of his new life in the United States.

Before He Terrorized a Country

On July 17, 1966, a boy by the name of Rubén Oseguera Cervantes was born in a small town in Michoacán. His family grew avocadoes in Tierra Caliente. Today, the region is better known for its drug production. Cervantes lived a normal life for a rural Mexican boy, dropping out of school in the fifth grade to help support his impoverished family. Like many Mexicans then and now, he got a job in the industry of drug trafficking to do this. At just fourteen years old, he began guarding crops of marijuana.

Little is known of this period in Cervantes's life. He reappeared in the public record in 1986. At nineteen years old, he was arrested in San Francisco when he was caught in possession of a gun and stolen property. According to

Nombre:	Nemecio Oseguera Cervantes y/o Rubén Aceguera Cerv Nemesio Oseguera Ramos, alias "El Mencho"
Estatus:	Probable Responsable
Monto de Recompensa:	2,000,000
Acuerdo:	A/102/2011
Zona de Operación:	Jalisco
Alias:	El Mencho
Seudónimo:	
Organización Delictiva:	
Delitos:	Delincuencia organizada y acopio de armas de fuego
Descripción de su actividad delictiva:	

El Mencho is one of the most wanted fugitives in the world.

Univision, Cervantes spent the next year frequently crossing the border and smuggling drugs. He became involved in the manufacture and sale of methamphetamine during this period. Thus far, Cervantes's biography reads like that of many teens who make a few wrong turns in life. But he was about to reach a new level of notoriety.

After serving three years in an American prison, he returned to Mexico and got a job as a state police officer. He later joined a DTO, the Milenio cartel, and rose through the ranks. In 2009, with the arrest of the cartel's leader, Cervantes assumed command. He rebranded the organization as the Cartel Jalisco Nueva Generación, or CJNG). By this time, he was known by his nickname, El Mencho. His brutality was unprecedented—a difficult feat in the violent world of Mexican DTOs.

He focused on methamphetamine production and smuggling. El Mencho also expanded his territory rapidly when El Chapo was extradited to the United States. Today, he is one of the most wanted men in Mexico. As of January 1, 2018, he is one of only three DEA "Top Wanted Fugitives." (The other two are the head of the Sinaloa cartel and a man still wanted for the murder of DEA agent Camarena in 1985.)

El Mencho's early life is telling. While cartel heads tend to be older men rather than teens, they often get their start in the criminal life from an exceptionally young age. However, unlike many of the children and teens who work for him, El Mencho had a choice about whether he led a life of crime and violence. Many young recruits today are only given the choice between killing or being killed by DTOs like CJNG.

Recruits North of the Border

DTOs do not just need recruits in Mexico, they also need people in the United States to do their bidding. Their criminal networks stretch uninterrupted across national borders. Just as in Mexico, in the United States, there is a need for all sorts of cartel workers. These roles include drug transporters and killers for hire.

JOURNALISTS FIGHT BACK

It is nearly impossible for the average citizen to fight back against Mexico's DTOs. They wield immense power and influence, and they are quick to use heinous acts of violence to silence any criticism. Nevertheless, many Mexican journalists go to work every day and report on the atrocities happening around them. This is one of the few ways that citizens can resist the DTOs; however, they do so at their own peril. Mexico is regularly ranked as one of the most dangerous places in the world to be a journalist. Journalists are targeted by DTOs as well as corrupt officials and police officers for speaking the truth.

One journalist who paid with her life for her defiance of DTOs was María del Rosario Fuentes Rubio. A doctor in Tamaulipas, she hid her identity online behind the handle Felina and a picture of Catwoman. She was an administrator of a site that warned local residents about drug cartel violence. She also personally urged victims to come forward and denounce their abusers. This enraged the cartels. They responded by threatening her life on social media.

When the cartels finally found out del Rosario's identity, they kidnapped her. They then posted a picture of her from her Twitter account, followed by a picture of her body after they murdered her.

Journalist Javier Valdez Cárdenas promotes his book *Orphans of the Drug Wars* months before his murder.

Del Rosario is just one of the many Mexican journalists killed for their work. Most murders go unsolved—journalists allege this is due to the involvement of local government officials and police in many of them. In 2017 alone, six journalists in Mexico were killed. When a journalist was murdered on March 23, 2017, award-winning journalist Javier Valdez Cárdenas tweeted, "Let them kill us all, if the sentence for covering this hell is death. No to silence." His brave sentiment is reflected in the acts of the Mexican press each day, although he was murdered less than two months later by unknown gunmen.

The Story of a Drug Mule

Cesar is one teen who was recruited while living in the United States. He lives in the border town of Eagle Pass, Texas. Like many young recruits, he was introduced to the criminal life through a friend.

When he was just twelve years old, Los Zetas recruited Cesar through two other young boys. They asked Cesar if he would like to work for the cartel. Initially, Cesar declined and said he did not want to work for Los Zetas. However, it quickly became apparent he had no choice in the matter. One of the boys told him he would regret it if he did not go with them on their next mission.

For the next year, Cesar did what Los Zetas asked him to do. This involved transporting drugs and cash across the border, by both driving across secured border crossings and walking across undefended parts of the Rio Grande. He also transported drugs within Texas from the border to the nearby city of San Antonio.

Cesar was paid for his work for Los Zetas, but he was constantly asked to perform new tasks for the DTO. One day, he and his friends were picked up by members of the cartel and driven to a remote ranch. A boy had gotten a call asking him to do something, and he had refused, saying he could not do it right then. In front of the other teens, a member of Los Zetas slit his throat and decapitated his body. Los Zetas wanted to make it clear that refusing to follow orders was not an option.

Despite this display of violence, Cesar finally had enough of his life working for the cartel. He called his boss and told him he was done. The man said he was going to come pick Cesar up and kill him. However, when he arrived at Cesar's house, he just pointed a gun at Cesar's head and laughed. He told Cesar he was not actually going to kill him, but he would kill his family if he refused to work.

Cesar agreed to transport a shipment of marijuana the next day. This time, Cesar was finally caught when he tried to cross the border. Since he was so young, he was soon released on probation. Luckily, Cesar's arrest led to his freedom from Los Zetas. A high-ranking member of the cartel who had met Cesar before called him to ask what had happened. When he heard that Cesar wished to leave, he was willing to allow it and told Cesar's boss to let him quit.

It seemed like Cesar had put that terrible chapter of his life behind him, although the horror of the violent acts he had witnessed stayed with him. But just two years later, Cesar received a phone call from a rival DTO, the Gulf cartel. They wanted Cesar to work for them and provide intelligence on Los Zetas. Cesar refused their requests until one day they called him and said, "We are coming for you. No need to hide."

Cesar texted his girlfriend and probation officer to say goodbye. Luckily for him, his probation officer called the police, and they went to his house. They took him into custody, and he escaped with his life.

American *Sicarios*

American teens are recruited to do more than just carry drugs across the border. They are also trained as *sicarios*. When cartels decide that people north of the border must be killed, it is often Americans who are used to do the killing.

Two of the most famous American *sicarios* are Gabriel Cardona and Rosalio Reta, childhood friends from Laredo, Texas. When they were arrested in the United States, their stories of brutality and violence shocked the country. Laredo's homicide rate is reported to have dropped by half after their capture. Their story was published by journalist Dan Slater in the book *Wolf Boys: Two American Teenagers and Mexico's Most Dangerous Drug Cartel*.

Gabriel Cardona became involved in low-level crime after dropping out of high school. He stole cars in Laredo and drove them across the border to sell them. Additionally, he trafficked guns across the border. One day, when he was trying to sell a stolen jeep in Nuevo Laredo, the Mexican city just south of

Rosalio Reta (*left*) and Gabriel Cardona (*right*) after their capture.

Laredo, he was captured by a group of armed men dressed in black who suspected he was working for a rival cartel. Their leader interrogated him and was impressed by Cardona's calm behavior (he was on sedatives at the time). It turned out that the man who captured Cardona was Miguel Treviño, the leader of Los Zetas. After determining that Cardona actually worked for a member of Los Zetas, not an enemy, Cardona was invited to a training camp for the cartel.

At the camp, Cardona was taught how to fire a number of different weapons as well as other skills that were useful for someone in his line of work. He practiced jumping between moving vehicles and shooting at a fleeing target. The recruits, about seventy people in all, also practiced killing.

Captured members of the Sinaloa cartel were used as live targets for practice.

After he completed his training, Cardona became a *sicario* for Los Zetas in Mexico. He was given $500 a week just to be ready for a mission. When he killed, he was given $10,000 for each victim. Since he worked in the territory of Los Zetas, he operated with impunity. On one occasion, he killed a victim in a diner while the police guarded the exterior for him outside. The police also disposed of the bodies of his victims for him—a job they were paid to do.

Cardona's luck ran out when he was commissioned to take the war against the Sinaloa cartel into the United States. As an American, he was a natural choice. But north of the border, he would not be above the law. Cardona later spoke of his confidence during his murder spree: "It gives you that sense that you could do anything without being touched and having that sense of power. You think that it's not going to end because it just keeps coming."

Cardona and the ring of killers he led killed at least five people in Texas before they were stopped. After being arrested, he pled guilty to seven murders, including two in Mexico, and received a life sentence in prison. In an interview with CNN, Cardona was unrepentant. He said, "I'm a really good person. It just happened." When asked how many people he killed in all, he could not remember, responding, "I have no idea. It's a violent world." He later estimated he had murdered at least thirty people.

Like Cardona, Rosalio Reta attended a training camp run by Los Zetas. But unlike Cardona, he claimed he had no choice. At the age of just thirteen, he says he was taken to a remote ranch in Mexico, handed a gun, and told by Miguel Treviño to kill a man. He says it was clear that if he refused, he would be killed as well. Many years later, he remembered, "I knew that my life had just changed forever. That's a day that I'm never going to be able to forget. After that, I didn't have no life."

Reta later joined Cardona's squad of killers in Texas. He was much younger than Cardona and was arrested when he was just sixteen years old. Nevertheless, he received thirty- and forty-year prison sentences for his crimes.

When he was interviewed by police, Reta admitted that he soon developed a taste for killing. He said, "There were others to do it, but I would volunteer. It was like a James Bond game. Anyone can do it, but not everyone wants to. Some are weak in the mind and cannot carry it in their conscience. Others sleep as peacefully as fish."

However, Reta later expressed remorse for his crimes. During an interview, he said, "I've come to regret everything I've done. I couldn't take it anymore. It was real hard for me. I wasn't living my life."

Female Recruits

There is little doubt that Mexican DTOs are run primarily by and for men. The clear majority of cartel leaders and their supporters are male. However, there are also a significant number of women who are involved in cartel life. According to experts, the number of female recruits has increased in recent years. Some women have little choice in the matter and are trafficked by the cartels—forced to work as prostitutes and sometimes even held captive as prisoners. Even when they are not forcibly held, there is often nowhere for them to run to when the reach of cartels is so far. But other women willingly join the cartels for money and fame.

One of the most famous female *sicarios* is named Juana, or "La Peque" ("The Little One"). She was born in the state of Hidalgo, and from a young age, she found herself on the wrong side of the law. She later told the press that, "Ever since I was a little girl I was a rebel, and then became a drug addict and an alcoholic." When she was just fifteen years old, she had a child and turned to prostitution to support herself. That is how she first encountered the world of the cartels.

She was recruited to be a *halconeo* (falcon) for Los Zetas. Her job was to look out for Mexican police and soldiers and warn the cartel of their movements. In jail, she recalled that if she failed in her duties, she was tied up and fed only one taco a day. While she was working as a *halconeo*, she witnessed a man beaten to death by cartel enforcers. At the time, she was upset, and later said, "I remember feeling sad and thinking I did not want to end up like that."

Before long, she was the one killing the cartel's opponents. She went to work as a *sicario* for Los Zetas. She was eventually captured by the police and imprisoned in Baja California—a Mexican state just south of the border of the American state of California. She was catapulted into the headlines when she gave a startling confession to authorities. She claimed to have not only killed and beheaded victims, but also to have bathed in and drunk their blood, among other indignities.

The Queen of the Pacific

Women have also risen to the highest levels of DTOs. The most well-known female cartel leader is Sandra Ávila Beltrán. Since a tuna-fishing vessel carrying nine tons of cocaine off the coast of California was linked to her, she has been called *La Reina del Pacífico*: the Queen of the Pacific.

Ávila was born into the world of drug trafficking. Her uncle was Miguel Angel Felix Gallardo—the founder of the Guadalajara cartel, one of the earliest major DTOs, as well as the man responsible for the murder of DEA agent Camarena.

Sandra Ávila Beltrán in 2012, when she was extradited to the United States to face charges of cocaine trafficking

As a result, her childhood was marked by incredible wealth. She attended private schools and went on frequent trips to American amusement parks like Disneyland.

But she also witnessed the darker side of cartel life. When she was just thirteen years old, she saw a shootout. Later in life, she recalled the violence of this period, "People walked the streets with pistols at the waist with musicians walking and playing behind them. At dawn you heard the music, the shootouts, it was when they killed the people."

At first, Ávila tried to avoid getting involved in the family business. She studied to be a journalist at a university in Guadalajara. But it was not that easy to escape the criminal lifestyle. She was kidnapped by a jealous boyfriend who was connected to the cartel world—like she was. After her release, she left Guadalajara and abandoned her studies. She returned to the world of the cartels.

Over the next decades, she rose through the ranks and became a major player in the scene of Mexican DTOs. When she was just twenty-one years old, she was conducting business with Amado Carillo Fuentes, known as "El Señor de los Cielos" ("Lord of the Skies"). Carillo was one of the most important traffickers of the era. He got his start transporting Pablo Escobar's cocaine to the United States with a fleet of private jets. Additionally, Ávila became a personal friend of Guzmán and dated a top Sinaloa cartel leader. Ávila was also married twice to major drug traffickers; both were killed while conducting business. Throughout her career, Ávila was a major player in the drug-trafficking business and an important link between different organizations in Mexico and Colombia.

In 2002, Ávila's luck began to turn. Her son was kidnapped by a rival cartel, and she paid a $5 million ransom for his safe return. This outrageous payment brought her to the attention of Mexican authorities. In 2004, a Mexican band released a song about her titled *"Fiesta in la Sierra"* ("Party in the Mountains"). In the song, Ávila goes to an exclusive party that can only be reached by private airplane or helicopter. The hit song increased her profile even more.

Finally, Ávila was arrested in 2007. She was convicted of laundering billions of dollars that were involved in drug smuggling between Mexico and Colombia. She spent the next seven years in prison, mostly in Mexico, although she was briefly extradited to the United States as well. In 2015, she was released. In her interviews with the media, she has refused to condemn the drug trade in Mexico and the violence that accompanies it. Instead, she says it is just "a business which has not been legalized," and compares narcotics traffickers to alcohol salesmen during Prohibition.

DTOs ON SOCIAL MEDIA

Since the days of Pablo Escobar, DTOs have tried to whitewash their actions in the eyes of the people. Escobar and Guzmán, among others, did this by cultivating a Robin Hood image of taking from the rich and giving back to the poor of their communities.

Today, DTOs have expanded to social media to try to justify their acts and inspire new recruits to join them. They post images of their huge amounts of money and heavy weaponry. Gold-plated guns, sports cars, private planes, exotic pets like lions and tigers, and palatial estates are common themes among the pictures posted by the top leadership level of DTOs. Among the lower ranks, selfies with guns glamorize violence.

These social media accounts glorify life as a drug trafficker, making it easier for DTOs to find new recruits for their organizations. Of course, the typical foot soldier has little chance of owning a private plane or multimillion-dollar mansion.

DTOs also use their social media presence to justify their actions. They often point a finger at corrupt politicians in their posts, implying that the elected officials are the real crooks, not them. They also insult rival DTOs and sometimes post images and video of the horrific violence they inflict on rivals.

The scene of a murder in Culiacán is cordoned off as investigators begin their work.

CHAPTER FOUR

MEXICO'S TEEN CASUALTIES

Across Mexico, the proliferation of DTOs and gangs has led to a sharp uptick in violence since the beginning of the Mexican Drug War in 2006. This violence has affected people all over the country from all walks of life.

It is important to remember that much of the violence and crime in Mexico is restricted to certain areas. Places like Tierra Caliente are considered some of the most dangerous in the world, with murder rates rivalling active war zones. But other parts of Mexico are quite safe and are still popular tourist attractions. The US Department of State gives a detailed breakdown of current travel advisories for each state in Mexico. Some entire states are considered unsafe for any travel, while other states are entirely safe. In some areas, certain roads and towns are considered unsafe due to their use by DTOs, while other areas are generally secure.

Spreading Drugs and Violence

The demand for illegal drugs in the United States, the rise of DTOs, and the violence of the Mexican Drug War have all led to very negative consequences in Mexican society. The rising tide of violence and massive supply of drugs moving northwards have altered daily life for many teens across the country.

The trafficking of drugs has led to a sharp increase in drug use in Mexico. In 2002, just 4.1 percent of Mexicans between the ages of twelve and sixty-five reported using drugs in a Mexican Health Ministry Survey. In 2016, this number had jumped to 9.9 percent—more than doubling in fifteen short years.

Increasingly, the drugs produced for the American market have instead stayed inside of Mexico. Towns along the border are inundated with cheap drugs, and drug use has become more and more common among residents. Nevertheless, drug use in Mexico is still dwarfed by drug use in the United States. In the United States, approximately 10 percent of Americans have used drugs in the past month

The US Coast Guard seizes a massive cocaine shipment discovered on a cargo ship.

alone. That is higher than the percentage of Mexicans who had used drugs in their entire lives.

The proliferation of drugs and the social problems drugs and violence cause, like broken families and poverty, have led to increased violence at all levels of society, not just among cartel members. Young people are bombarded with images of violence in the media and sometimes in their daily lives if they live in an insecure area. This in turn leads to more violence.

One young man who suffered from this kind of commonplace violence was Nicolás Barrera. He did not have ties to any gang or cartel. He was just an ordinary young man who had plans and dreams for the future and his whole life ahead of him. All of that changed one day when he went to a friend's party. An argument started between him and another man. At first, everything seemed fine. But then a group of men showed up and murdered him in front of dozens of witnesses. The murderers were never caught, so their reason for the violence is not known. They may have been gang or DTO members, or simply other youths who thought they were defending the honor of their friend.

Whatever the motive, Nicolás was killed in cold blood that day, and his family continues to suffer. They want justice, but that is unlikely in Mexico. Approximately 98 percent of murders in the country go unsolved. This impunity stems in part from the drug war, which leads to the corruption of law enforcement as well as many *sicarios* being above the law.

Nicolás's father Oscar lamented the country's situation after his son's slaying: "These kids just show up and kill each other. It's so rough. Imagine reaching that extreme where these youths are killing each other. There's a total lack of security." This insecurity has deadly consequences for many each year.

Indigenous People

Mexico is an extremely diverse nation. When the Spanish first arrived in 1519, the territory of Mexico was inhabited by many different indigenous people. They spoke different languages and had different cultures, although some groups shared many beliefs and traditions. Over the next five centuries, the Spanish and indigenous people lived together in modern-day Mexico. Their cultures, ideas, languages, and traditions blended together—with Spanish becoming the lingua franca of the diverse country. Most of Mexico's people descend from both indigenous and Spanish ancestors.

However, there are still large groups of indigenous people in Mexico. They have preserved their culture from before the Spanish even arrived in the New World. The exact number of indigenous people depends on how you define them. In 2015, 21.5 percent of Mexico's population self-identified as indigenous on the country's census. But only 6.5 percent spoke an indigenous language. It is likely that some indigenous people hide their ancestry on the census due to the discrimination in some areas of the country against indigenous people.

One of the more than sixty indigenous groups that call Mexico home is the Rarámuri. They live in northwestern

A Rarámuri family relaxes at home in the border state of Chihuahua.

Mexico in the state of Chihuahua, which borders the United States. Like many indigenous groups, they kept their culture alive by fleeing into remote areas as the Spanish conquered the country. Their communities are still located in the remote mountains of the Sierra Madre Occidental mountain range.

As is the case with other indigenous peoples in Mexico, the Rarámuri are under intense pressure from DTOs in their homeland. They are forced through violence to work for drug traffickers in industries like poppy cultivation. One Rarámuri village, El Manzano, was a typical community just a few years ago. The thirty-four families that resided there made their living farming corn and raising livestock. They practiced their indigenous beliefs by gathering together and performing ceremonies.

That all changed when members of a Mexican cartel came to the town. The Rarámuri were given a choice: grow poppies or die. They stopped practicing their indigenous beliefs, opting instead to hide indoors due to the trucks full of cartel gunmen that would drive through town.

Some Rarámuri refused to do as the cartel said. One was Mexican teen Benjamín Sánchez, who would not tend the poppies that had replaced the corn his family used to farm. In response, the cartel came to town and killed him. The residents of the town were helpless before the indiscriminate violence of the cartel.

Benjamín's father talked to Vice News about what life was like before his son was murdered: "They wanted the locals to work for them and join their group. Almost everyone is put to work [growing poppy] on their own land. That group controls several municipalities." The cartels later tried to kill the older Sánchez on two occasions, but he escaped both times. In one shootout, another one of his sons was shot three times but survived.

Finally, the Sánchez family left the village that had been their home for so long. There was no other choice. Sánchez described his feelings upon leaving his ancestral home: "You miss everything. We were born there, our parents called it their homeland, and so did our grandfathers. We are left with nothing."

Violence Against Migrants

The number of people from Central America seeking refuge in the United States has grown in recent years. This increase in the number of migrants is largely due to factors at home. Gang violence in countries like Guatemala, Honduras, and El Salvador is a constant threat to residents. In 2015, the homicide rate in El Salvador reached 104 per 100,000 people—meaning 0.1 percent of the country's population was murdered that year alone. As a result, many people try to reach the United States so that they will not be killed or forcibly conscripted to join a gang. Unfortunately, many are not legally allowed to enter the United States—or any other country. They are left with a choice: stay home and try to live amidst the violence, or migrate illegally. Many choose the second option to try to save their own lives as well as the lives of their family members.

Most of these migrants come from a region known as the Northern Triangle of Central America (NTCA), an insecure, impoverished region at the crossroads of El Salvador, Guatemala, and Honduras. They make the long journey out of their homelands and across Mexico with the hope of then crossing into the United States. However, this dangerous trek is just as fraught with violence as the region they leave behind.

Migrants ride atop cargo trains on their journey northward. The dangerous trains are known as La Bestia ("The Beast").

Leading nongovernmental organization Doctors Without Borders explains the hardship of their lives:

> *For millions of people from the NTCA region, trauma, fear, and horrific violence are dominant facets of daily life. Yet it is a reality that does not end with their forced flight to Mexico. Along the migration route from the NTCA, migrants and refugees are preyed upon by criminal organizations, sometimes with the tacit approval or complicity of national authorities, and subjected to violence and other abuses—abduction, theft, extortion, torture, and rape—that can leave them injured and traumatized.*

This crisis was spotlighted in the press in 2014, when the number of unaccompanied minors reaching the US border quickly doubled. Without their parents—who were often deceased or too poor to make the journey at the same time—these minors presented a major problem for the American government. There were no suitable detention centers to hold them while their cases were heard individually by immigration judges. Some were deported. Others were eventually placed in foster care.

In response to the 2014 crisis, the United States launched a propaganda campaign in the NTCA region to discourage further migration, warning residents that they would likely not be allowed to stay in the United States, even if they survived the perilous journey. The American government also worked with Mexico to stop more teens south of the US border and have them deported from Mexico. As a result, the crisis ended, although the number of unaccompanied minors fleeing from Central America to the United States each year remains in the thousands.

With the crackdown by American authorities, many migrants have instead decided to stay in Mexico rather than continue to the United States. Unfortunately, they often find themselves in the middle of the Mexican Drug War. Cartels aim to recruit them—often through force—to serve as expendable soldiers. Without even legal residency in the country, they are exceptionally vulnerable to exploitation since they are unable to turn to the police for help.

Witness to the San Fernando Massacre

In the summer of 2010, a group of migrants was making its way through Mexico to the United States. They hoped to make a new life for themselves there, free of the poverty and violence that they were forced to live with at home. The migrants were from a variety of different countries south of Mexico including Ecuador, Brazil, El Salvador, and Honduras.

But most of them never reached the United States. They were passing through the Mexican state of Tamaulipas, the last place on their route before the border. It is also the heart of Los Zetas' territory. Luis, a nineteen-year-old from Ecuador, later told Mexican authorities what happened next.

On Saturday, August 22, at about 10 o'clock at night, we were surrounded by three cars. Around eight well-armed people got out and put us in two other cars. They took us to a house. We stayed there one day. Then, they took us to another side. There, they tied us four by four with our hands behind our backs. Afterwards, they threw us face down, and I heard gunshots. I thought it was something outside, but no, they were shooting my friends. Then another man came in shooting at us, killing everyone else. When they finished firing, they left. I waited two minutes before I got up and left the house. I walked all night. I arrived at a house that was very far away. Two men came out, I asked for their help ... but they did not want to help me. Then I saw a light ... I continued walking towards the little light. I ran about another 10 kilometers [6.2 mi]. I arrived in pain, asking for help, but nobody wanted to help me. I kept walking and walking until it was daytime, and at about seven in the morning I saw the Mexican marines. I reached them and asked for help.

The Mexican marines launched a raid on the compound that Luis described. They killed three cartel gunmen, but many others escaped. One marine died in the firefight as well. After the battle, the authorities found seventy-two bodies—fifty-eight men and fourteen women. Just as Luis said, they had been bound and shot to death.

The migrants had been killed because they did not have the money to pay for their release, and they refused to work for Los Zetas. Their story is not unique. The very next year, 194 migrants were massacred in the very same region of Mexico, the San Fernando Valley.

Sexual Slavery

In Mexico, there are more than thirty thousand missing people according to official sources. There is no doubt that the true number of the disappeared is much higher. Many are likely dead—victims of the Mexican Drug War whose bodies may never be discovered or laid to rest.

Some of the missing are kept in slavery, mostly by DTOs. One of the main reasons for this is prostitution. Girls and women, as well as some boys, are kidnapped by the cartels and kept in captivity. Clients pay to have sex with them, and the cartels keep all the money. The captives are kept under the control of the cartels through violence and fear. Clients sometimes do not even know the prostitute is a sex slave and think they are a prostitute by choice.

Lupita, a woman from a rural community, talked to the *Guardian* about what she saw in her hometown before she left. The area was controlled by a DTO—and no one was safe from them. She recalled the first time a group of armed men arrived:

> *When they got out of the van all we could see were the machine guns in their hands. They wanted to know where the pretty one was, the girl with*

FLEEING THE VIOLENCE

Widespread drug-related violence affects the daily lives of millions of Mexicans. Many are forced from their homes as a result. Typically, refugees from the violence have two choices: relocate inside of Mexico or emigrate to another country, like the United States.

Contrary to the stereotype, many Mexicans who decide to leave the country due to violence do so legally. They invest large sums of money in the United States in return for a visa. Many Mexican business owners and entrepreneurs follow this route when they grow tired of the drug-related violence of their home country.

The options for less affluent Mexicans are much worse. If they want to cross the border, they will likely have to rely on a *coyote*—an illegal guide. After giving a great deal of money to the coyote, there is no guarantee they will be led safely across the border. Many are abandoned along the way, sometimes in the unforgiving desert that forms the border at places. Others are assaulted and robbed on the journey when they are completely at the mercy of the gang leading them across.

Due to this danger, the number of Mexicans trying to cross into the United States illegally has declined in recent years. Instead, many Mexicans who are forced to leave their homes because of violence simply relocate within Mexico.

freckles. We all knew who that was. They took her and she was still holding her doll under her arm when they lifted her into the van like a bag of apples. This was more than 12 years ago. We never heard from her again.

The men kept coming back and taking more girls. The villagers resorted to digging holes in the ground and hiding their children in them when the men approached, but eventually the holes were discovered. Lupita eventually moved to Mexico City rather than remain in her hometown.

Tragically, such situations happen regularly across Mexico and even in neighboring countries. Girls from Nicaragua are kidnapped by cartels and transported across the border to be sex slaves. This happened to Daniela when she was twenty years old. For the next nine years, she was kept in captivity by Los Zetas. They showed her videos of other slaves who tried to escape being tortured to death. She was even asked to kill a fellow sex slave. When she refused, he was tortured and left for dead in front of her. She believes this was a test to see if she would make a good *sicario* after she was too old to be as profitable as a sex slave. In the end, she escaped with the help of someone she refuses to name. Her savior also helped her remove a GPS chip the cartel had implanted in her foot to track her movements. When she told Mexican authorities of her ordeal, they sent her back to Nicaragua. It was only after a nongovernmental organization (NGO) helped her that an investigation was started.

The Cartel's Opponents

To fight the brutal, powerful DTOs in Mexico, their opponents have sometimes turned to criminal means themselves. Nowhere is this more apparent than the Mexican state of Michoacán. Michoacán lies in the Tierra Caliente ("hot land") region of Mexico. This region is a hotbed of DTO activity due to its favorable climate for growing marijuana and opium as well as its transportation links to ports and other Mexican states. Of the three states that have territory in Tierra Caliente, Michoacán in particular

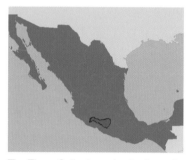

The Tierra Caliente region is shown in red on this map.

has a reputation for lawlessness and violence. It is one of the five Mexican states (of thirty-four total) that the US State Department recommends travelers visit under no circumstances—the same level of warning that war zones like Afghanistan and Syria receive.

To combat the drug violence and often corrupt local politicians who do little about it, some citizens of Michoacán took the law into their own hands. They formed self-defense groups (*autodefensas*) to fight back against cartel gunmen. Local business owners and farmers took up arms and hunted down members of the cartels, dispensing their own justice. The self-defense groups succeeded in driving the cartels out of their cities but soon turned to criminal activities themselves.

The Mexican government initially tried to recruit the militias to their side, giving them uniforms. This move further blurred the lines between government forces and criminal groups as some *autodefensas* began producing drugs and taking over cartel businesses. The alliance between Mexican law enforcement and self-defense groups soon largely broke down. Government forces tried to disarm the groups, who sometimes fought back. Adding more complications, rival DTOs sometimes aided the self-defense groups in their fight against their enemies, and some self-defense group leaders were well-known former cartel members.

Today, the future of *autodefensas* is unclear. They do not hold the same sway in Michoacán as they did a couple of years ago at the peak of their power. However, they still routinely threaten to rearm if the government does not do more to end the violence in the state and combat DTOs.

THE PIRATE OF CULIACÁN

One teen who rose to internet stardom in Mexico was Juan Luis Lagunas Rosales. Born to a poor family in Sinaloa, he grew up under the care of his grandmother after both his parents abandoned him. When he was fifteen years old, he dropped out of high school and moved to Culiacán, Sinaloa. He found a job washing cars to make ends meet. Like some teens who find themselves independent at such a young age, he started partying and drinking excessively. He made videos of his drinking habits and uploaded them to social media, where they went viral. As a result, he gained a massive following online.

Life seemed to be going well for Lagunas—with the exception of the heavy drinking that he was trying to get under control. At only seventeen years old, he had just signed a record deal. He talked to his friends about drinking less and making changes in his life. But one day, while recording a video for social media, he insulted El Mencho while he was intoxicated.

Soon after, he went out to a bar in Jalisco. As he and his friends hung out there, gunmen entered the bar and opened fire at Lagunas. The teen was shot more than a dozen times for the drunken insult. Police had to use his tattoos to identify his body. His fame could not protect him from the violence of the Jalisco New Generation Cartel.

In addition to the murky world of *autodefensas*, it is an unfortunate fact that Mexican security forces themselves are often implicated in brutal acts of violence. According to Human Rights Watch, "security forces have been implicated in repeated, serious human rights violations—including extrajudicial killings, enforced disappearances, and torture— during efforts to combat organized crime." Extrajudicial killings refer to the act of executing a person without a trial. It is criminal behavior for law enforcement to engage in. Meanwhile, enforced disappearances are the imprisonment of people outside of regular judicial channels. It is often done to hide evidence of torture and extrajudicial killings.

The killing or enforced disappearance of DTO or gang members is bad in and of itself. However, the situation is much worse when the corruption of some Mexican security force members is considered. Mexican DTOs have successfully bribed and threatened some police and military members to do their bidding. It is likely that this is behind some of the killings that security forces engage in—they are crimes committed to aid the cartels rather than combat them.

The 2014 Iguala Mass Kidnapping

One case exemplifies the collusion between Mexican DTOs and law enforcement. In 2014, forty-three students of

Ayotzinapa Rural Teachers' College were kidnapped and disappeared in Iguala, Guerrero. They were all young men who were just beginning their lives. Many of them were still teens. What exactly happened to the forty-three students remains a mystery.

The students were traveling in a number of buses near Iguala when local police began to pursue them. The police officers shot at one bus, forcing it to pull over. One student was shot in the head and went into a coma. Twenty more students were arrested and driven away by the police—they were never seen again. More students gathered at the scene of the attack and began speaking to the press there when indiscriminate gunfire broke out. A witness described the scene, "We ran in the other direction. You could hear cries and moans and the bursts of gunfire that kept going." Two

In 2016, protesters marched in Mexico City to demand the return of the missing students.

students were killed in the shooting. During the same time frame, other buses were stopped, and all the students aboard them were escorted away by police.

Once the chaos came to an end, friends and relatives realized that forty-three students were missing. Many were last seen in police custody. Protests broke out across Mexico at the brazen disappearance of the students, and demonstrators demanded their safe return. No trace of the students was found at first, but it soon became clear that their safe return was unlikely. The Mexican federal government and human rights groups began investigating what exactly happened— and they came to different conclusions. It is clear that local police were involved. It is very likely that they handed over the students to a local DTO, Guerreros Unidos, to carry out the murders and dispose of the bodies. Whether federal police and the Mexican army were also involved is a matter of controversy.

The motive for the mass disappearance (and almost certainly murder) is also somewhat unclear. Iguala's mayor is often blamed. It is proposed that he was worried the students were going to demonstrate at an event where his wife was due to give a speech. If true, the banal reason for mass murder underscores the impunity the mayor thought he had.

In the days after the disappearance, a mass grave was discovered with many burnt human remains. It turned out that these were yet more unidentified victims of violence and not the missing students. So far, only one bone fragment has been found in Guerrero that was linked to a missing student. It is likely that their families will never know for certain what happened to their loved ones.

Police Shootings

In the highly charged atmosphere of the drug war, violence sometimes occurs where it is least expected. This is the case on the US border of Mexico, where there have been a number of high-profile shootings of Mexican teens by US border patrol agents.

In 2010, fifteen-year-old Sergio Hernandez was shot by an agent on the American side of the border while he was on the Mexican side. The agent claimed it was an attempted illegal crossing and rocks were being thrown at him. The boy's lawyers contend he was playing a game with a friend where they would run up and touch the border fence, in plain view of the major crossing. They did not believe this would be met with deadly force.

The shooting was captured on video and reveals the children were not throwing rocks. Instead, it shows an unarmed Hernandez desperately seeking cover behind a pillar as shots ring out. There was insufficient room for him to hide, and he was shot in the head and killed. No criminal charges were filed against the agent after law enforcement rallied to support him. Hernandez's parent filed a civil suit against the agent, seeking damages. Thus far, the case is still tied up in the courts as lawyers for the border agent argue that an American court has no jurisdiction over the case. Meanwhile, Hernandez's lawyers argue that this tactic means Americans can shoot Mexicans across the border with impunity.

In yet another case, sixteen-year-old Elena Rodriguez was killed by a border agent in Nogales, Mexico. Once again, the case revolves around the issue of rock throwing. There is video footage of Rodriguez throwing rocks at agents from a great distance to cover the smuggling of marijuana across the border. However, all agents but one simply took cover, since the rocks were thrown from fifty feet away and unlikely to inflict great harm. Only one agent approached the fence and fired through it, killing Rodriguez. Furthermore, he fired thirteen of sixteen shots at Rodriguez while Rodriguez lay on the ground, wounded and unmoving. In all, Rodriguez was shot ten times.

In this case, the border agent involved is being prosecuted in the United States. However, as of February 2018, the trial has still not taken place, even though the shooting occurred in 2012. Justice for victims of violence in Mexico is rarely quick on either side of the border.

Us Border Patrol agents confiscate over 400 lbs (181 kg) of marijuana that was brought over the Rio Grande.

CHAPTER FIVE

SOLVING TERROR

As the Mexican Drug War stretches on for more than a dozen years, solutions to the problem are difficult to find. Civilian casualties remain stubbornly high. The DTOs themselves have not bowed under military pressure in any way. Indeed, they are arming themselves with even more weaponry and fighting back more fiercely—shooting down their first helicopter in 2015 and then another one in 2016.

The kingpin strategy of seeking to arrest high-level cartel leaders appears misguided to most experts given its history. Spikes in violence are often observed after the arrest of a major leader as others jockey to take his or her place. When cartels are weakened to the point of dissolving, others grow stronger, or new ones spring up to fill the void. The situation for Mexican civilians caught in the crossfire remains the same.

However, there are some strategies that experts think may help. Fighting corruption and strengthening the rule of law in Mexico may at the very least drive the drug trade underground and out of the streets. Likewise, trying to end the root causes that lead to young people joining criminal organizations, like poverty and delinquency, might help put an end to the conflict. There have been many different proposals by experts to end the violence, considering the current situation on the ground.

Decreasing the Demand for Drugs

One of the most common ideas to decrease violence south of the border is to drive down the demand for illegal drugs north of the border. Unfortunately, the insatiable demand for drugs in the United States seems as intractable a problem as the drug-related violence it spawns in Mexico. The hope is that lower drug use in the United States may make drug trafficking in Mexico less profitable, driving violence down as DTOs make less money and fight less fiercely over smuggling routes.

However, drug use in the United States continues to climb. In 2002, 8.3 percent of Americans aged twelve or older reported using illegal drugs in the past month. By 2008, the number had climbed to 9.4 percent, and in 2016 it stood at 10.3 percent. Drug use seems to be increasingly steadily. These statistics are supported by the rising number of drug overdoses sweeping through the United States.

Given the seeming futility of lessening the demand for illegal drugs in the United States, many people have argued that some drugs—most often marijuana—should simply be legalized instead. The reasoning is that cartel profits will decrease, and the US government will raise more revenues by taxing it. Some states have legalized it, but DTOs in Mexico seem to have taken the move toward legalization in stride. They have simply increased production of much more lucrative—and dangerous—drugs like heroin, methamphetamine, and fentanyl.

The countries of Latin America have likewise made some moves to legalize drugs in recent years in order to curb drug-trafficking violence. In 2017, Mexico announced that selling some marijuana products, though not the leaf itself, would become legal in 2018. It remains to be seen whether this will be followed by a greater push for expansive marijuana legalization.

Nevertheless, many experts do not see legalization as a real solution to the problem of Mexican cartels at this stage in their evolution. While DTOs were originally built solely around drug production and smuggling, they have moved into industries other than drug trafficking in recent years. Extorting businesses—even major ones in Mexico—and kidnapping for ransom have become commonplace. Experts worry that legalizing drugs might simply encourage DTOs to continue these practices.

Fighting Corruption and Strengthening the Rule of Law

The most promising way to curb drug-related violence in Mexico is also one of the most difficult: reducing political corruption and reinforcing the rule of law in the country. Corruption and the weak rule of law, leading to impunity for DTOs and criminals, are two sides of the same coin. It is the ability to buy off law enforcement and politicians that lets cartels operate without worrying about consequences. They know their freedom can be bought. Many journalists have published that they suspect Guzmán simply bribed the government to be let out of prison in 2015, and the tunnel that was shown to the press was simply a cover story. The Queen of the Pacific opined that such an escape involved at the very least a paid-off Cabinet member—someone in the president's inner circle.

An NGO called Transparency International ranks countries according to their perceived level of corruption. In 2016, they ranked Mexico 123rd of the 176 countries they surveyed. For comparison, Denmark was number one while the United States was eighteen and Canada was nine. Corruption is a fact of daily life for many Mexicans, who must routinely pay government officials and law enforcement. Transparency International's 2017 poll found that 51 percent of Mexicans reported they had paid a bribe in the past twelve months so that they could receive a basic government service.

Meanwhile, crimes typically go unpunished. Perpetrators are rarely caught, and human rights abuses by the military and law enforcement are well-documented. Another NGO, Human Rights Watch, has collected many interviews with people convicted of crimes whose guilt is very suspect. These people report being tortured into confessions by those meant to protect them. Despite regular false convictions, most crimes are never solved.

Experts agree that fighting corruption and ending the current era of impunity for DTOs is the most meaningful step toward ending drug-related violence that Mexico can take. DTOs will continue to wage bloody wars in valuable areas like Ciudad Juárez until it is not in their financial interest to do so. Thus far, given the fact that they are often aided by local law enforcement rather than hunted by them, it has been in their interest to continue their bloody wars.

Doing the Opposite

While most experts agree that strengthening the rule of law is the only way to decrease violence, some people argue for the exact opposite. Most recently, Mexican presidential candidate Andrés Manuel López Obrador took this position. He said that he would consider giving DTOs amnesty for their crimes if victims and the families of victims were willing. When speaking to reporters, he said, "We'll propose it. I'm analyzing it. What I can say is that we will leave no issue without discussion if it has to do with peace and tranquility"

The idea of a ceasefire with DTOs has a long history. Indeed, most people suspect such a deal was in place in Mexico before President Calderón began the drug war in 2006. In Colombia, a deal resembling amnesty was reached with Pablo Escobar when he surrendered to authorities with the promise that he would serve no more than five years in a luxury prison of his own design. There, the result was a brief lull in the violence before it reignited with his escape.

Many experts do not even believe a deal is possible with DTOs in Mexico anymore. Such a deal would require a unified block of cartel leaders to negotiate with. With the balkanization of cartels and the arrest of leaders like Guzmán, the DTOs have splintered into many factions led by local leaders. It is unlikely there is anyone powerful enough for the Mexican government to negotiate with who could promise— and deliver—peace.

Ending Poverty

Many people believe that there is a link between poverty and drug-related violence, although the exact relationship is not always clear. Many drug traffickers were quite wealthy before becoming involved in the business, and the vast majority of Mexicans living in poverty avoid the cartels.

About 44 percent of Mexicans live in poverty according to the Mexican government. This is based on a number of factors like access to education, family income, house size, and access to electricity and sufficient food. Approximately 7 percent of the population lives in extreme poverty, which means they are unable to afford the basic necessities of life like food and health care.

This extraordinarily high poverty rate is accompanied by a massive amount of wealth concentrated in Mexico's upper class. Fourteen billionaires call the country home. This makes Mexico score very poorly on measures of income inequality—the gap between what the rich and poor earn. According to the Organization for Economic Co-operation and Development (OECD), Mexico has the

THE ATF GUNWALKING SCANDAL

For Mexican DTOs, one of the simplest ways to get guns is to buy them in the United States. Gun control laws are generally lax, especially in some border states. It is possible for people to walk into a gun store and buy dozens of assault rifles to be used by transnational criminal organizations. These purchases are known as straw purchases—when someone buys a weapon to give it to someone else. Straw purchases are illegal because they result in the intended recipient of the gun avoiding a background check.

The Bureau of Alcohol, Tobacco, Firearms, and Explosives (ATF) generally arrests straw purchasers if they catch them. However, in a series of operations between 2006 and 2011, the ATF did not arrest some straw purchasers who bought guns for Mexican DTOs. Instead, agents allowed the guns to "walk" across the border into the hands of the DTOs. It was hoped that by tracing the guns they might find the leaders of the cartels who arranged for their purchase.

Unfortunately, many of the thousands of guns sold to DTOs were lost rather than traced. They began to turn up at crime scenes around Mexico. Then, in December 2010, two guns that had walked were found at the murder scene of US Border Patrol Agent Brian Terry. News of the scandal soon broke as

US Border Patrol agents attended a memorial service for Brian Terry on January 21, 2011.

ATF agents leaked information about the gunwalking—many agents had opposed the program even before Terry's murder.

The scandal rocked President Barack Obama's administration. Attorney General Eric Holder, who oversaw the ATF, was held in contempt by Congress. When Guzmán was captured years later, a massive .50 caliber rifle—capable of stopping a car or helicopter—was found in his hideout and traced back to the gunwalking scandal.

highest inequality of any of its thirty-five member countries. However, OECD members tend to be developed countries, and many developing countries outside of the OECD score worse than Mexico.

Security analyst Duncan Wood at the Wilson Center argues that this inequality is at the center of the drug-trafficking problem in Mexico. "You combine inequality with ineffective government," says Wood, "and you have a very toxic situation where organized crime is an alternative for young men—but it's also a force that very few governmental actors are willing to confront."

Youth alienated from society, who grow up in poverty and see wealth all around them on television and social media, turn to DTOs and gangs. While the poverty rate in Mexico is dropping, the number of people who live in poverty in Mexico is staying roughly the same due to an increasing population. Many NGOs operate in Mexico trying to fight poverty, but their work is just beginning. The lack of security due to DTOs and government corruption make it an uphill battle.

Former Gang Members Work to End Violence

Juan Pablo García is one man who was born into poverty and then fell into gang life when he was a youth. He told the *Guardian*, "I grew up in a very poor neighborhood. We didn't even have water or basic services. After my dad abandoned us, I wanted to earn money on the streets to support my mum, but I ended up getting involved with gangs." But García managed to turn his life around and leave the gang. He now devotes his life to ending the violence.

In 2011, he founded an NGO he named Born to Triumph. It aims to prevent young people from joining gangs and DTOs in his home city of Monterrey. He and his staff, who are almost all former gang members, go out into the city and talk to gangs that are operating there. They try to convince them to sign peace deals with neighboring gangs and go to education centers to reintegrate with society.

This outreach by former gang members is a promising way to stop the violence. Other NGOs around the country run by local community members also have the same goal: an end to the violence that wracks their communities. García told the *Guardian*, "You can't fix this with more soldiers and police. We need dialogue, love, and affection. That's what empowers young people, telling a kid that he's important and has a future."

The War Drags On

Despite the work of enterprising Mexicans like García, the current situation in Mexico is quite bleak. DTOs still operate with relative impunity. The arrest of kingpins like

Guzmán has led some DTOs to splinter, but they continue operating in decentralized groups that are harder to combat. Additionally, they turn to even more violent activities like extortion and kidnapping to turn a profit as the drug-trafficking scene becomes crowded with more and more DTOs. October 2017 was the deadliest month in Mexico since modern records began being kept. There are no signs that the violence is abating.

Mexican DTOs are increasingly targeting younger and younger children for recruitment. Many have not even reached their teenage years when they are forced to begin working for the cartels. The recruitment of American teens across the border also continues.

There is little that people in the United States can do to end the violence. Government corruption in Mexico is a difficult problem to tackle. One of the few meaningful things that US citizens can do is refuse to buy illicit drugs. Drug money is the fuel that drives the conflict in Mexico. It funds the violence and terror that grip the country. Without the demand for drugs in the United States, the violence never would have begun there.

FIGHTING MACHISMO WITH SOCCER

Machismo—or extreme pride in being a man—has a long history in Mexico's culture. There is societal pressure for men to act macho, and gender stereotypes are often strict. Many people link this macho culture to the high rate of violence that Mexican women suffer, often from their boyfriends or husbands. Femicide, the murder of women due to their gender, is the most extreme manifestation of machismo. It is a common occurrence in some parts of Mexico, especially Ciudad Juárez on the border and the state of Mexico near the center of the country.

Guadalupe Garcia is one woman who is fighting back against machismo in Mexico. She saw the effect of gender-based violence firsthand. Her mother grew up an orphan after her grandfather beat her grandmother to death. Garcia turned to soccer at a young age "as an act of rebellion." Traditionally, women in her conservative community were dissuaded from playing the sport, which was seen as a manly activity. Now, as an adult, Garcia started a soccer club for young women in her community. Its very existence is a challenge to machismo. Garcia explains the value of playing for the girls she coaches, "What we do is reclaim our human rights by doing this sport. It must be known that women can also occupy these roles in society, and it also ends up empowering women."

CHRONOLOGY

Mid-1970s

In Colombia, Pablo Escobar begins running a massive drug trafficking organization that centers around smuggling cocaine into the United States.

1980s The Gulf cartel begins trafficking drugs.

1995 Joaquín "El Chapo" Guzmán takes over control of the Sinaloa cartel and begins expanding its power. It is soon the most feared DTO in the world.

2006 The Mexican Drug War begins when Mexican President Felipe Calderón orders soldiers to fight the cartels.

2009 The Jalisco New Generation Cartel (Cartel Jalisco Nueva Generación, CJNG) is founded and quickly expands.

2010 Los Zetas violently break away from their former employers, the Gulf cartel, and begin operating independently.

2017 Guzmán is extradited to the United States to face criminal charges, sparking even more violence in Mexico as cartels fight to fill the power vacuum.

GLOSSARY

autodefensas Self-defense militias that communities form to fight DTOs when law enforcement is unwilling or unable to combat the cartels.

cartel A group of producers who work together to keep prices high. Drug cartels do not meet this definition and, therefore, most academics use the term drug trafficking organizations (DTOs) instead. However, the media still uses the term cartel to refer to DTOs around the world, as do cartels themselves.

CJNG Cartel Jalisco Nueva Generación or Jalisco New Generation Cartel; one of the two most powerful DTOs in Mexico, originally part of the Sinaloa cartel but later became independent.

developed countries Countries with relatively high levels of wealth and economic infrastructure.

drug mule A person who smuggles drugs for DTOs.

DTO Drug Trafficking Organization; the term that academics and experts use to refer to drug cartels.

fentanyl A synthetic opioid (meaning it can be produced in a lab rather than through processing opium poppies); it is about fifty times as strong as heroin.

Guadalajara The second most–populous metropolitan area in Mexico behind the capital.

Guerrero One of Mexico's thirty-one states. Part of the state is in the Tierra Caliente region, which is a major area of drug production and smuggling.

Gulf cartel One of the oldest cartels. Its roots can be traced back to the Prohibition Era, although the modern organization dates to the 1980s.

halconeo Lookout for law enforcement used by criminal groups.

impunity Exemption from punishment, often due to corruption in law enforcement or politics.

lingua franca The common language that a society or country has when its different ethnic groups may speak different languages at home.

Los Zetas A DTO that was part of the Gulf cartel in the 2000s but broke away in 2010. It was created by former special forces soldiers and is renowned for its violence.

Mexican Drug War The militarized conflict between the Mexican government and Mexican DTOs that began in December of 2006 with a government offensive and continues to the present day.

Michoacán One of Mexico's thirty-one states. The state frequently makes headlines for the *autodefensas* that operate in it due to the widespread drug-related violence that takes place there.

NGO Nongovernmental Organization; organizations that are independent of the government and often nonprofits.

opioid A class of drugs that are primarily used for pain relief in medical settings. Recreationally, they are used for the euphoria they cause.

sicario The Spanish word for hit man; it is used to denote drug cartel assassins.

Sinaloa cartel The leading Mexican cartel since at least 2011. It was headed by notorious cartel kingpin Joaquín "El Chapo" Guzmán until his extradition to the United States in 2017.

Tierra Caliente A region composed of parts of Michoacán, Guerrero, and the state of Mexico that is a center of drug production and trafficking and a frequent scene of cartel clashes.

FURTHER INFORMATION

Books

Engdahl, Sylvia. *The War on Drugs*. New York: Greenhaven
   Publishing, 2009.

Reilly, Mary Jo, Leslie Jermyn, and Michael Spilling.
   Cultures of the World: Mexico. New York: Cavendish
   Square, 2012.

Websites

The Shifting Toll of America's Drug Epidemic

https://www.economist.com/blogs/
graphicdetail/2017/10/daily-chart-18

The *Economist* presents infographics that show the age,
substance, and geographical breakdown of the rising
number of drug overdoses.

A Timeline of El Chapo's Reign on the Run

https://www.cnn.com/2016/07/01/world/a-
history-of-el-chapos-reign/index.html

CNN gives details about Joaquín Guzmán's life and multiple
escapes from prison as he led the Sinaloa cartel.

Videos

"How Fentanyl is Making the Opioid Epidemic Even Worse"

https://www.vox.com/videos/2017/7/27/16049840/fentanyl-opioid-epidemic-worse

Embedded in an article on *Vox*, this video outlines the history of the opioid crisis in the United States and discusses the rising danger of fentanyl.

"No Way Out: Drug Cartels Recruit Kids for Life"

https://www.cnn.com/2017/05/09/americas/mexico-second-deadliest-conflict-2016/index.html

CNN interviews a few teens in Texas who have worked for Mexican cartels.

BIBLIOGRAPHY

Agence France-Presse. "Mexican Girls Fight Violence with Boy's Own Game—Football." *Jamaica Observer*, November 9, 2017. http://www.jamaicaobserver.com/ sports/mexican-girls-fight-violence-with-boys-8217-own-game-8212-football_116463?profile=1513.

Bedard, Paul. "Report: Nearly all, 98.8%, of Illegal Drugs Shipped to the U.S. from Mexico." *Washington Examiner*, November 22, 2016. http://www.washingtonexaminer. com/report-nearly-all-998-of-illegal-drugs-shipped-to-us-from-mexico/article/2607990.

CDC. "Provisional Counts of Drug Overdoses, as of 8/6/2017." 2017. https://www.cdc.gov/nchs/data/health_ policy/monthly-drug-overdose-death-estimates.pdf.

Clement, Jennifer. "Mexico's Lost Daughters: How Young Women Are Sold into the Sex Trade by Drug Gangs." *Guardian*, February 8, 2014. https://www.theguardian. com/world/2014/feb/08/mexico-young-women-sex-trade-drug-gangs.

Contreras, Evelio. "Inside the Life of a Drug-trafficking Teen." CNN, August 13, 2015. http://www.cnn.com/2015/08/12/ us/inside-the-life-of-a-drug-trafficking-teen/index.html.

Eells, Josh. "The Brutal Rise of El Mencho." *Rolling Stone*, July 11, 2017. https://www.rollingstone.com/culture/features/the-brutal-rise-of-el-mencho-w491405.

Franklin, Jonathan. "Queen of the Cartels: The Most Famous Female Leader of Mexico's Underworld Speaks Out." *Guardian*, May 16, 2016. https://www.theguardian.com/society/2016/may/16/mexico-drug-cartels-famous-female-leader-sandra-avila.

García, Gustavo Castillo. "Sobreviviente de la Masacre Afirma Que Los Secuestrados Fueron 76; Dos, Desaparecidos." *La Jornada*, September 3, 2010. http://www.jornada.unam.mx/2010/09/03/index.php?section=politica&article=015n1pol.

Grillo, Ioan. *El Narco: The Bloody Rise of Mexican Drug Cartels*. London: Bloomsbury Publishing, 2011.

———. "Mexican Drug Smugglers to Trump: Thanks!" *New York Times*, May 5, 2017. https://www.nytimes.com/2017/05/05/opinion/sunday/mexican-drug-smugglers-to-trump-thanks.html.

Grinberg, Emanuella. "El Paso School a Haven along Violent Border." CNN, May 20, 2009. http://www.cnn.com/2009/US/05/20/elpaso.juarez.school/index.html.

Heinle, Kimberly, Octavio Rodríguez Ferreira, and David
     A. Shirk. *Drug Violence in Mexico: Data and Analysis
     through 2016*. San Diego, CA: Justice in Mexico, 2017.

Hopkins, Anna. "American Teenager Was Trampled to
     Death During Mexican Nightclub Shooting: Vacationing
     18-year-old from Denver Is Named as One of Five Dead
     amid Fears Cartel Wars Have Arrived in Resort Popular
     with Americans." *Daily Mail*, January 17, 2017. http://
     www.dailymail.co.uk/news/article-4126782/American-
     teenager-trampled-death-nightclub-shooting.html.

Jones, Nathan P. "Understanding and Addressing Youth
     in Gangs in Mexico." Working Paper, Woodrow
     Wilson Center for International Scholars, 2013. http://
     wilsoncenter.org/publication/understanding-youth-
     gangs-mexico.

Langton, Jerry. *Gangland: The Rise of the Mexican Cartels
     from El Paso to Vancouver*. Hoboken, NJ: Wiley, 2011.

McGahan, Jason. "She Tweeted Against the Mexican
     Cartels: They Tweeted Her Murder." *Daily Beast*,
     October 21, 2014. https://www.thedailybeast.com/she-
     tweeted-against-the-mexican-cartels-they-tweeted-
     her-murder.

Partlow, Joshua. "Mexico's Drug Trade Hits Home." *Washington Post*, December 21, 2017. https://www.washingtonpost.com/graphics/2017/world/mexico-s-drug-traffic-is-now-hitting-home/?utm_term=.d481d3c81d2f.

Sheridan, Mary Beth. "Drug War Sparks Exodus of Affluent Mexicans." *Washington Post*, August 26, 2011. https://www.washingtonpost.com/world/national-security/drug-war-sparks-exodus-of-affluent-mexicans/2011/08/19/gIQA6OR1gJ_story.html?utm_term=.0214c0f48c10.

Slater, Dan. *Wolf Boys: Two American Teenagers and Mexico's Most Dangerous Cartels*. New York: Simon & Schuster, 2016.

Stewart, Scott. "Mexico's Cartels Will Continue to Splinter in 2017." *Stratfor*, February 2, 2017. https://worldview.stratfor.com/article/mexicos-cartels-will-continue-splinter-2017.

Tucker, Duncan. "'I Can't Believe How I Used to Live:' From Gang War to Peace Treaties in Monterrey." *Guardian*, February 22, 2017. https://www.theguardian.com/cities/2017/feb/22/gang-war-peace-treaties-monterrey-mexico.

US Library of Congress. Congressional Research Service. *Mexico: Organized Crime and Drug Trafficking Organizations*, by June S. Beittel.

VICE News. "Cartels are Displacing Indigenous Group That's Lived in this Mexican State for Centuries." May 20, 2016. https://news.vice.com/article/cartels-are-displacing-an-indigenous-group-thats-lived-in-this-mexican-state-for-centuries.

Winslow, Don. "El Chapo and the Secret History of the Heroin Crisis." *Esquire,* August 9, 2016. http://www.esquire.com/news-politics/a46918/heroin-mexico-el-chapo-cartels-don-winslow.

Woody, Christopher. "In Mexico's 'Hot Land,' Citizen Self-defense Forces and Criminal Groups May Be Gearing Up for More Violence." *Business Insider*, December 11, 2016. http://www.businessinsider.com/autodefensas-causing-violence-in-guerrero-and-michoacan-in-mexico-2016-12.

INDEX

ABOUT THE AUTHOR

Derek Miller is a writer and educator from Salisbury, Maryland. Miller is the author of more than a dozen books, including *The Fourth Estate: The African American Press* and *Fighting for Their Country: Minority Soldiers Fighting in the Korean War*. When he is not writing, researching, or teaching, Miller enjoys traveling with his wife.